The
Book
Lover's
Book
Of
Quotes

Rocky Henriques

compiler

ISBN-13: 978-1981590766

ISBN-10: 1981590765

Carpenter's Corner Press,
Utica, Mississippi

The quoted ideas expressed in this book are not, in all cases, exact quotations, as some have been edited for clarity and brevity. In all cases, the author has attempted to maintain the writer's original intent. In many cases, quoted material for this book was obtained from secondary sources. While every effort was made to ensure the accuracy of these sources, the accuracy cannot be guaranteed. For additions, deletions, corrections or clarifications in future editions of this text, please contact the compiler.

For
my dad,
Stanley M. Henriques, Sr.

who taught me
the love of reading

Contents

Dedication

When I was a child, my family lived in Mobile, Alabama, in a neighborhood where there were lots of boys who loved to play baseball. Most of the time that was in a flat, empty field just in front of our house. In the thick heat of a south Alabama summer, we would rise with excitement in the morning, as if we hadn't just played baseball several hours just the day before. We would wolf down a bowl of cereal, grab our gloves, bats and baseballs and head out the back door to wait for the other kids to show up. We would play in the coolness of the early morning, but never noticed when the temperature rose and the sweat dripped from our bodies. We loved to play, and we played all morning, stopping only to retrieve a foul ball which had rolled under a car in the neighborhood, or to fish the ball from the ditch at the edge of the field, or to grab a quick drink of water from the garden hose at one of the houses nearby.

Then we would take a break for lunch, which usually consisted of peanut butter-and-jelly sandwiches., at least at our house. After lunch, we had the entire afternoon ahead of us, which for us in the hot summer, allowed for very few options. We were too far from the beach, and no one had a swimming pool, so we would climb the branches of mimosa trees, hike through the nearby woods and catch crayfish ("crawdads") and minnows. Occasionally, if the heat coming off Mobile Bay wasn't too oppressive, the empty field would call to us, and we would head back to the field, where we played still more baseball, barefooted, without bases or a backstop. Our feet were hard and calloused and we rarely wore shoes.

And we would play until it was too dark to see. Or until our mothers called us in for supper. But that play didn't resume immediately after we wiped the peanut butter from our faces. Not at my house.

You see, Dad had other ideas. He required that the boys in his house spend the hour right after lunch reading. We could read anything we wanted to, but we had to read. The other boys went on with their afternoons, and we would catch up later.

In those days, the Mobile Public Library had what were called "bookmobiles," and Mom frequently would take us to visit one of them at a shopping center a couple of miles away. The library usually had reading programs during the summer, in which we earned little trinkets for reading a certain number of books. I still have some of them!

Stepping up into the bookmobile, I would take a deep breath of the fragrance unique to a bunch of books piled up in a small space. I would load up with the maximum number of books, and look forward to the time when I could lose myself in them. Sometimes I would read well past the required hour, being engaged too much in the story or the characters to put the book down. Early on, I discovered the problem many book lovers have, of telling themselves they will read "just one more page," or "until I reach the end of this chapter." Many times, the other boys would go on about their play without me.

I read anything I could get my hands on— even the back of the cereal box in the early mornings. *The World Book Encyclopedia* and the *Childcraft* books were fair game as well. It happened often that I would close a book after finishing it, lay it against my chest, and feel a little sadness that I had come to the end of it. I didn't know at the time that was a common experience to readers everywhere in all times.

To this day, one of my favorite childhood memories is reading on the floor in front of the large window in the living room, or on a bed next to a window, with a pouring thunderstorm emptying itself on our little house. Now these long years later, I still want to reach for a book whenever I hear it thunder.

Kate DiCamillo once wrote, "Reading should not be presented to children as a chore or duty. It should be offered to them as a precious gift."

Dad said, "Read an hour," and I saw it as the gift it was. I found that I loved reading as much as I loved playing baseball, so my memories of those humid summer days include a morning of baseball followed by as much of the afternoon as I could steal from chores so I could bury my nose in yet another book.

We later moved to Jackson, Mississippi, where Dad converted an extra bedroom in our home into a study with a full set of built-in, floor-to-ceiling bookshelves. Those shelves were twelve inches deep so they could hold the old LP record albums, but that depth meant that the rest of the space had double rows of books.

That room became for me a place of solitude, of comfort, a place where I could think, read and study, surrounded by books read and yet-to-be-read.

Even now, floor-to-ceiling bookshelves are the norm in my own house, each of them filled with books I've collected over the years—again, read and yet-to-be read, some occupying a spot on the shelf as a reference book. Just their presence, silent and patiently waiting for me, still comforts me.

So my dad is the one I credit with teaching me the love of reading, with instilling in me the understanding that even though I should pursue an education, I was ultimately the one in charge of what I learned by the choice of books I allowed into my life.

I tried my best to pass these ideals along to my children, by surrounding them with books just as you did us, and I am proud to say they are readers as well. And now your great-grandchildren, who never got to meet you, would rather spend an afternoon reading than almost anything else.

So thank you, Dad, for the priceless gift you gave me. Even now, years after you left us, I'm not sure you ever realized how valuable it was to me.

With great love and very fond memories, I dedicate this book to you, Stanley M. Henriques, Sr.

Bibliophile

A lover of books;
someone who finds joy and peace
of mind while holding a quality book.

1
Why Should We Read?

Reading gives us some place to go when
we have to stay where we are.

Mason Cooley

I read because one life isn't enough, and
in the page of a book I can be anybody.

Richard Peck

Sometimes you read a book, and it fills you with this weird evangelical zeal ... and you become convinced that the shattered world will never be put back together unless and until all living humans read the book.

John Green

There are worse crimes than burning books. One of them is not reading them.

Ray Bradbury

Clean out a corner of your mind and creativity will instantly fill it.

Dee Hock

Reading is important, because if you can read, you can learn anything about everything and everything about anything.

Tomie dePaola

When you reread a classic you do not see more in the book than you did before; you see more in you than there was before.

Clifton Fadiman

When we read we may not only be kings and live in palaces, but, what is far better, we may transport ourselves to the mountains or the seashore, and visit the most beautiful parts of the earth, without fatigue, inconvenience, or expense.

John Lubbock

If you cannot read all your books, at any rate handle, or as it were, fondle them—peer into them, let them fall open where they will, read from the first sentence that arrests the eye, set them back on the shelves with your own hands, arrange them on your own plan so that you at least know where they are. Let them be your friends; let them at any rate be your acquaintances.

Winston Churchill

The end of reading is not more books but more life.

Holbrook Jackson

Never read a book through merely because you have begun it.

John Witherspoon

I never remain passive in the process of reading: while I read I am engaged in a constant creative activity, which leads me to remember not so much the actual matter of

the book as the thoughts evoked in my mind
by it, directly or indirectly.

Nicolas Berdyaev

Reading is a socially acceptable form of
hallucination.

Laura Furman

We use books like mirrors, gazing into them
only to discover ourselves.

Joseph Epstein

It is chiefly through books that we enjoy
intercourse with superior minds . . . . In the
best books, great men talk to us, give us their
most precious thoughts, and pour their souls
into ours.

William Ellery Channing

The reading of all good books is like a
conversation with the finest men of past
centuries.

Rene Descartes

Some books are meant to be tasted, others to
be swallowed, and some few to be chewed
and digested; that is, some books are to be
read only in parts; others to be read but not

curiously; and some few to be read wholly, and with diligence and attention.

Francis Bacon

By taking down one of these volumes and opening, it one can call into range the voice of a man far distant in time and space and hear him speaking to us, mind to mind, heart to heart.

Gilbert Highet

Reading is everything. Reading makes me feel like I've accomplished something, learned something, become a smarter person. Reading makes me smarter. Reading gives me something to talk about later on. Reading is the unbelievably healthy way my attention deficit disorder medicates itself. Reading is escape, and the opposite of escape; it's a way to make contact with reality after a day of making things up, and it's a way of making contact with someone else's imagination after a day that's all too real. Reading is grist. Reading is bliss.

Nora Ephron

Think before you speak. Read before you think.

Fran Lebowitz

Reading furnishes the mind only with materials of knowledge; it is thinking that makes what we read ours.

John Locke

You think your pain and your heartbreak are unprecedented in the history of the world, but then you read. It was books that taught me that the things that tormented me most were the very things that connected me with all the people who were alive, or who had ever been alive.

James Baldwin

Some people read to confirm their own hopelessness. Others read to be rescued from it.

Anais Nin

To read a book is to hold an entire world in the palm of your hand. That world is unique to you; no two readers can ever inhabit the same world.

Arthur Schopenhauer

Reading is the sole means by which we slip, involuntarily, often helplessly, into another's skin, another's voice, another's soul.

Joyce Carol Oates

By reading the writings of the most interesting minds in history, we meditate with our own minds and theirs as well. This to me is a miracle.

Kurt Vonnegut

Writing and reading decrease our sense of isolation. It's like singing on a boat during a terrible storm at sea. You can't stop the raging storm, but singing can change the hearts and spirits of the people who are together on that ship.

Anne Lamott

To read is to fly: it is to soar to a point of vantage which gives a view over wide terrains of history, human variety, ideas, shared experience, and the fruits of many inquiries.

A. C. Grayling

The unread story is not a story; it is little black marks on wood pulp. The reader, reading it, makes it live: a live thing, not a story.

Ursula K. Le Guin

Whenever you read a good book somewhere in the world a door opens to allow in more light.

Vera Nazarian

One glance at a book and you hear the voice of another person, perhaps someone dead for 1,000 years. To read is to voyage through time.

Carl Sagan

On rare occasions there comes along a profound original, an odd little book that appears out of nowhere, from the pen of some obscure storyteller, and once you have read it, you will never go completely back to where you were before. The kind of book you might hesitate to lend for fear you might miss its company. The kind of book that echoes from the heart of some ancient knowing, and whispers from time's forgotten cave that life may be more than it seems, and less.

Edmund J. Banfield

A book is not complete until it's read. The reader's mind flows through sentences as through a circuit--it illuminates them and brings them to life.

E. L. Doctorow

Dinosaurs didn't read. Look what happened to them.

An Unknown Book Lover

Reading is dreaming with open eyes.

An Unknown Book Lover

Finally reading for your own pleasure, in places quiet or loud, in relative comfort, preferably without interruption, the book you've been meaning to read for months (perhaps years), and which has been on your shelf, waiting for you to have time.

An Unknown Book Lover

Reading can seriously damage your ignorance.

An Unknown Book Lover

Books don't change people; paragraphs do, sometimes even sentences.

John Piper

To reach the top we stand on the books we've read.

An Unknown Book Lover

The author who benefits you most is not the one who tells you something you did not know before, but the one who gives expression to the truth that has been dumbly struggling in you for utterance.

Oswald Chambers

Just saw a person reading my favorite book ...
it's like a book recommending a person.

An Unknown Book Lover

Reading a book is like re-writing it for
yourself. You bring to a novel, anything you
read, all your experience of the world. You
bring your history and you read it in your own
terms.

Angela Carter

Man reading should be man intensely alive.
The book should be a ball of light in one's
hand.

Ezra Pound

All the secrets of the world are contained in
books. Read at your own risk.

Lemony Snicket

There are books full of great writing that
don't have very good stories. Read sometimes
for the story. Don't be like the book-snobs
who don't do that. Read sometimes for the
words--the language. Don't be like the play-it-
safers that won't do that. But when you find a
book that has both a good story and good
words, treasure that book.

Stephen King

We read five words on the first page of a really good novel and we begin to forget that we are reading printed words on a page; we begin to see images.

John Gardner

The first book we fall in love with shapes us every bit as much as the first person we fall in love with.

Laura Miller

You can borrow a book, but you get to keep the ideas.

The National Reading Campaign

Books are cheaper than holidays and better than therapy. And you don't need to leave town or make an appointment.

Unknown

I read books because I love them, not because I think I should read books.

Simon Van Booy

I am part of everything that I have read.

Theodore Roosevelt

Reading is a discount ticket to everywhere.

Mary Schmich

No entertainment is so cheap as reading, nor any pleasure so lasting.

Lady Mary Wortley Montagu

Reading makes immigrants of us all. It takes us away from home, but more important, it finds homes for us everywhere.

Jean Rhys

The book to read is not the one that thinks for you but the one which makes you think.

Harper Lee

No matter how busy you may think you are, you must find time for reading or surrender yourself to self-chosen ignorance.

Confucius (verify)

Reading is not optional.

Walter Dean Myers

There are many little ways to enlarge your world. Love of books is the best of all.

Jacqueline Kennedy

You can find magic wherever you look. Sit back and relax, all you need is a book.

Dr. Seuss

I am a reader, not because I don't have a life, but because I choose to have many.

An Unknown Book Lover

A reader lives a thousand lives before he dies. The man who never reads lives only one.

George R. R. Martin

I do not read because I have renounced life; I read because one life is just not enough for me.

Abbas Al-Akkad

I would rather be poor in a cottage full of books than a king without the desire to read.

Thomas Babington Macaulay

The act of reading is a partnership. The author builds a house, but the reader makes it a home.

Jodi Picoult

Reading is an art form, and every man can be an artist.

Edwin Louis Cole

Good books don't give up all their secrets at once.

Stephen King

Buying a book is not about obtaining a possession, but about securing a portal.

Laura Miller

Reading is a means of thinking with another person's mind; it forces you to stretch your own.

Charles Scribner, Jr.

In reading great literature I become a thousand men and yet remain myself.

C. S. Lewis

Once you learn to read, you will be forever free.

Frederick Douglass

Books fall open, you fall in. When you climb out again, you're a bit larger than you used to be.

Gregory Macguire

Old books exert a strange fascination in me: their smell, their feel, their history, wondering who might have owned them, how they lived and what they felt.

Lauren Willig

There are worse crimes than burning books.
One of them is not reading them.

Ray Bradbury

I will never cease to be amazed by books.
Seriously. Just think about it: thousands of
people read the same book but in each one's
mind the characters look different and the
setting changes and we're all reading the same
thing but it's so unique to each of us. That is
insanely cool.

Unknown

The book to read is not the one that thinks
for you but the one which makes you think.

Harper Lee

When you reread a classic you do not see
more in the book than you did before; you see
more in you than there was before.

Clifton Fadiman

When we read we may not only be kings and
live in palaces, but, what is far better, we may
transport ourselves to the mountains or the
seashore, and visit the most beautiful parts of
the earth, without fatigue, inconvenience, or
expense.

John Lubbock

It is the books we read before middle life that do most to mold our characters and influence our lives.

Robert Pitman

Never read a book through merely because you have begun it.

John Witherspoon

The way a book is read—which is to say, the qualities a reader brings to a book—can have as much to do with its worth as anything the author puts into it. . . . Anyone who can read can learn how to read deeply and thus live more fully.

Norman Cousins

I never remain passive in the process of reading: while I read I am engaged in a constant creative activity, which leads me to remember not so much the actual matter of the book as the thoughts evoked in my mind by it, directly or indirectly.

Nicolas Berdyaev

In a very real sense, people who have read good literature have lived more than people who cannot or will not read. . . . It is not true that we can have only one life to live; if we can read, we can live as many more lives and as many kinds of lives as we wish.

S. I. Hayakawa

It is chiefly through books that we enjoy intercourse with superior minds . . . . In the best books, great men talk to us, give us their most precious thoughts, and pour their souls into ours.

William Ellery Channing

The reading of all good books is like a conversation with the finest men of past centuries.

Rene Descartes

By taking down one of these volumes and opening, it one can call into range the voice of a man far distant in time and space and hear him speaking to us, mind to mind, heart to heart.

Gilbert Highet

Reading is to the mind what exercise is to the body.

Joseph Addison

He that loves reading has everything within
his reach.

William Godwin

The reading of books, what is it but
conversing with the wisest men of all ages and
all countries.

Isaac Barrow

If we encountered a man of rare intellect, we
should ask him what books he read.

Ralph Waldo Emerson

When I read a book, I put in all the
imagination I can, so that it is almost like
writing the book as well as reading it - or
rather, it is like living it. It makes reading so
much more exciting, but I don't suppose
many people try to do it.

Dodie Smith

For one who reads, there is no limit to the
number of lives that may be lived, for fiction,
biography, and history offer an inexhaustible
number of lives in many parts of the world, in
all periods of time.

Louis L'Amour

Be as careful of the books you read, as of the company you keep; for your habits and character will be as much influenced by the former as the latter.

Paxton Hood

Reading is the life-saving water for our minds. Drink pure words as much as you need and remain alive.

Munia Khan

If you take a book into your hands, be it God's book, or any other useful good book, rely on God to make it profitable to you. Do not waste time reading unprofitable books. When you read, do so not out of vain curiosity but with love for God's kingdom, compassion for human beings, and the intent to turn what you learn into prayers and praises.

Matthew Henry

For all I know, writing comes out of a superior devotion to reading.

Eudora Welty

If one reads enough books one has a fighting chance. Or better, one's chances of survival increase with each book one reads.

Sherman Alexie

We should read to give our souls a chance to luxuriate.

Henry Miller

Read. Read anything. Read the things they say are good for you, and the things they claim are junk. You'll find what you need to find. Just read.

Neil Gaiman

A fondness for reading, properly directed, must be an education in itself.

Jane Austen

Reading is everything. Reading makes me feel like I've accomplished something, learned something, become a smarter person. Reading makes me smarter. Reading gives me something to talk about later on. Reading is the unbelievably healthy way my attention deficit disorder medicates itself. Reading is escape, and the opposite of escape; it's a way to make contact with reality after a day of making things up, and it's a way of making contact with someone else's imagination after

a day that's all too real. Reading is grist.
Reading is bliss.

Nora Ephron

Think before you speak. Read before you
think.

Fran Lebowitz

Never judge a book by its movie.

J. W. Eagan

Reading furnishes the mind only with
materials of knowledge; it is thinking that
makes what we read ours..

John Locke

You think your pain and your heartbreak are
unprecedented in the history of the world, but
then you read. It was books that taught me
that the things that tormented me most were
the very things that connected me with all the
people who were alive, or who had ever been
alive.

James Baldwin

Some people read to confirm their own
hopelessness. Others read to be rescued from
it.

Anais Nin

To read a book is to hold an entire world in the palm of your hand. That world is unique to you; no two readers can ever inhabit the same world.

Arthur Schopenhauer

A good book is all-consuming: part of it becomes you, and part of you becomes it.

Wisława Szymborska

If you only read the books that everyone else is reading, you can only think what everyone else is thinking..

Haruki Murakami

By reading the writings of the most interesting minds in history, we meditate with our own minds and theirs as well. This to me is a miracle.

Kurt Vonnegut

The unread story is not a story; it is little black marks on wood pulp. The reader, reading it, makes it live: a live thing, not a story.

Ursula K. Le Guin

Reading fiction is important. It is a vital means of imagining a life other than your own, which in turn makes us more empathetic beings. Following complex story lives stretches our brains beyond the 140 characters of sound-bite thinking, and staying within the world of a novel gives us the ability to be quiet and alone, two skills that are disappearing faster than the polar icecaps.

Ann Patchett

Whenever you read a good book somewhere in the world a door opens to allow in more light.

Vera Nazarian

Dinosaurs didn't read. Look what happened to them.

An Unknown Book Lover

Books build a stairway to your imagination.

Stifyn Emrys

Reading can seriously damage your ignorance.

Unknown

I trod new paths, entertained new thoughts, inhaled new scents, heard new sounds. I did all this without once leaving my chair.

William Dalton

To read is to fly: it is to soar to a point of vantage which gives a view over wide terrains of history, human variety, ideas, shared experience, and the fruits of many enquiries.

A. C. Grayling

Read the best books first, or you may not have a chance to read them at all.

Henry David Thoreau

The act of reading is a partnership. The author builds a house, but the reader makes it a home.

Jodi Picoult

2
The Joy of Reading

What a joy there is in a good book, writ
by some great master of thought, who
breaks into beauty as in summer the
meadow into grass and dandelions and
violets with geraniums and manifold
sweetness.

Theodore Parker

If the crowns of all the kingdoms of
Europe were laid down at my feet in
exchange for my books and my love of
reading, I would spurn them all.

Francois Fenelon

Good friends, good books and a sleepy
conscience: this is the ideal life.

Mark Twain

I have sought for happiness everywhere, but I
have found it nowhere except in a little corner
with a little book.

Thomas a Kempis

An ordinary man can surround himself with
two thousand books and thenceforward have
at least one place in the world in which it is
always possible to be happy.

Augustine Birrell

No matter what his rank or position may be,
the lover of books is the richest and happiest
of the children of men.

John Alfred Langford

Book love, my friend, is your pass to the
greatest, the purest, and the most perfect
pleasure that God has prepared for His
creatures. It lasts when all other pleasures
fade. It will support you when all other
recreations have gone. It will last until your
death. It will make your hours pleasant to you
as long as you live.

Anthony Trollope

Isn't it a joy—there is hardly a greater one—
to find a new book, a living book, and to
know that it will remain with you while life
lasts.

Katherine Mansfield

It had been startling and disappointing to me
to find out that storybooks had been written
by people, that books were not natural
wonders, coming up of themselves like grass.
Yet regardless of where they came from, I
cannot remember a time when I was not in
love with them—with the books themselves,
cover and binding and the paper they were
printed on, with their smell and their weight
and with their possession in my arms,
captured and carried off to myself. Still
illiterate, I was ready for them, committed to
all the reading I could give them.

Eudora Welty

My early and invincible love of reading ... I
would not exchange for the treasures of India.

Edward Gibbon

That I can read and be happy while I am
reading, is a great blessing. Could I have
remembered, as some men do, what I read, I
should have been able to call myself an

educated man. But that power I have never possessed. Something is always left—something dim and inaccurate—but still something sufficient to preserve the taste for more. I am inclined to think that it is so with most readers.

Anthony Trollope

My books! I cannot tell you what they are to me—silent wealthy, loyal, lovers. I do thank God for my books with every fiber of my being.

Oswald Chambers

The love of reading enables a man to exchange the wearisome hours of life, which come to everyone, for hours of delight.

Montesquieu

Dreams, books, are each a world,
and books we know,
Are a substantial world, both pure and good.
Round these, with tendrils strong as flesh and blood,
Our pastime and our happiness will grow.

William Wordsworth

We read five words on the first page of a really good novel and we begin to forget that we are reading printed words on a page; we begin to see images.

John Gardner

The best moments in reading are when you come across something--a thought, a feeling, a way of looking at things--which you had thought special and particular to you. And now, here it is, set down by someone else, a person you have never met, someone even who is long dead. And it is as if a hand has come out, and taken yours.

Alan Bennett

You can find magic
Wherever you look.
Sit back and relax,
All you need is a book.

Dr. Seuss

Books are the perfect entertainment: no commercials, no batteries, hours of enjoyment for each dollar spent. What I wonder is why everybody doesn't carry a book around for those inevitable dead spots in life.

Stephen King

I trod new paths, entertained new thoughts,

inhaled new scents, heard new sounds. I did
all this without once leaving my chair.

William Dalton

I declare there is no enjoyment like reading.

Jane Austen

I would rather be poor in a cottage full of
books than a king without the desire to read.

Thomas Babington Macaulay

Sometimes you read a book so special that
you want to carry it around with you for
months after you've finished just to stay near
to it.

Markus Zusak

I love the solitude of reading. I love the deep
dive into someone else's story, the delicious
ache of a last page.

Naomi Shihab Nye

Reading a good book in silence is like eating
chocolate for the rest of your life and never
getting fat.

Becca Fitzpatrick

Book love is something like romantic love.
When we are reading a really great book,

burdens feel lighter, cares seem smaller.

Steve Leveen

The greatest gift is the passion for reading. It is cheap, it consoles, it distracts, it excites, it gives you knowledge of the world and experience of a wide kind.

Elizabeth Hardwick

That moment when you're reading a book and the whole world around you does not exist anymore.

David Avocado Wolfe

To sit alone in the lamplight with a book spread out before you, and hold intimate converse with men of unseen generations— such is a pleasure beyond compare.

Kenko Yoshida

There is nothing better than the feeling of opening the first pages of a much-anticipated book.

Unknown

With freedom, books, flowers and the moon, who could not be happy.

Oscar Wilde

Happiness is ignoring the world because
you're reading.

Unknown

The first thing that reading teaches us is how
to be alone.

Jonathan Franzen

The problem with reading a good book is that
you want to finish the book, but you don't
want to finish the book.

Unknown

A good book is never finished—it goes on
whispering to you from the wall.

Virginia Euwer Wolff

Some books you read. Some books you enjoy.
But some books just swallow you up, heart
and soul.

Joanne Harris

Oh, for a book
And a shady nook
Either indoors or out
With the green leaves
Whispering overhead
Or the street cries all about

Where I may read
At all my ease
Both of the new and the old
For a jolly good book
Whereon to look
Is better to me than gold.

John Wilson

The love of learning, the sequestered nooks,
And all the sweet serenity of books.

Henry Wadsworth Longfellow

When you read a line that is so well-written,
you just close the book and stare at the wall
for a minute.

An Unknown Book Lover

You know you've read a good book when you
turn the last page and feel a little as if you
have lost a friend.

Paul Sweeney

I declare there is no enjoyment like reading.

Jane Austen

You can't buy happiness, but you can buy
books and that's kind of the same thing.

An Unknown Book Lover

For some of us, books are as important as almost anything on earth. What a miracle it is that out of these small, flat, rigid squares of paper unfolds world after world after world, worlds that sing to you, comfort and quiet or excite you. Books help us understand who we are and how we are to behave. They show us what community and friendship mean. They show us how to live and die.

Anne Lamott

A half-read book is a half-finished love affair.

David Mitchell

What on earth could be more luxurious than a sofa, a book, and a cup of coffee.

Anthony Trollope

Wherever I am, if I've got a book with me, I have a place I can go and be happy.

J. K. Rowling

Read something today. There are few pleasures so rewarding as a warm fire and a good book.

Joseph Morgan

I have always been a reader; I have read at every stage of my life, and there has never been a time when reading was not my greatest joy. I still believe in stories. I still forget myself when I am in the middle of a good book. Books are for me, it must be said, the most important thing.

Diane Setterfield

There is more treasure in books than in all the pirate's loot on Treasure Island.

Walt Disney

The stories we love best live in us forever.

J. K. Rowling

What really knocks me out is a book that, when you're all done reading it, you wish the author that wrote it was a terrific friend of yours and you could call him up whenever you felt like.

J. D. Salinger

I declare after all there is no enjoyment like reading! How much sooner one tires of anything than of a book.

Jane Austen

There is no scent so pleasant to my nostrils as

that faint, subtle reek which comes from an ancient book.

Arthur Conan Doyle

If you don't like to read, you haven't found the right book.

J. K. Rowling

If a book is well written, I always find it too short.

Jane Austen

Picking five favorite books is like picking the five body parts you'd most like not to lose.

Neil Gaiman

Happiness is a new stack of unread library books.

An Unknown Book Lover

So if people ever look down upon you for crying for fictional characters, you should give them a gentle, pitying look and feel bad for them. If they've never cried for a fictional character, then they've never loved one (and what a joy that is). If they've never cried at a book, a movie, a piece of music, then they've missed one of the great pleasures life has to offer. Just because fiction does not contain things that are real doesn't mean it doesn't contain truth, and we find it through the alchemy of our tears.

Cassandra Clare

Books fall open, you fall in,
delighted where you've never been.
Hear voices not once heard before,
Reach world through world,
through door on door.
Find unexpected keys to things,
locked up beyond imaginings ...
True books will venture,
dare you out,
whisper secrets,
Maybe shout,
across the gloom to you in need
who hanker for a book to read.

David McCord

I wish I could erase my memory of some books just so I could read them for the first time all over again.

Unknown

When you read a book, the neurons in your brain fire overtime, deciding what the characters are wearing, how they're standing, and what it feels like the first time they kiss.

No one shows you. The words make suggestions. Your brain paints the pictures.

Meg Rosoff

I have no time to waste on a book whose every sentence isn't a delight.

Viet Thanh Nguyen

No matter what his rank or position may be, the lover of books is the richest and happiest of the children of men.

John Alfred Langford

I have sought for happiness everywhere, but I have found it nowhere except in a little corner with a little book..

Thomas a Kempis

Book love, my friend, is your pass to the greatest, the purest, and the most perfect pleasure that God has prepared for His creatures. It lasts when all other pleasures fade. It will support you when all other recreations have gone. It will last until your death. It will make your hours pleasant to you as long as you live.

Anthony Trollope

What a joy there is in a good book, writ by

some great master of thought, who breaks
into beauty as in summer the meadow into
grass and dandelions and violets with
geraniums and manifold sweetness.

Theodore Parker

Isn't it a joy—there is hardly a greater one—
to find a new book, a living book, and to
know that it will remain with you while life
lasts.

Katherine Mansfield

That I can read and be happy while I am
reading, is a great blessing. Could I have
remembered, as some men do, what I read, I
should have been able to call myself an
educated man. But that power I have never
possessed. Something is always left—
something dim and inaccurate—but still
something sufficient to preserve the taste for
more. I am inclined to think that it is so with
most readers.

Anthony Trollope

Where is the human nature so weak as in the
bookstore?

Henry Ward Beecher

If a book is worth reading, it is worth buying.
John Ruskin

Never lend books, for no one ever returns them; the only books I have in my library are books that other folks have lent me.
Anatole France

A home without books is like a room without windows. A little library, growing every year, is an honorable part of a man's history. It is a man's duty to have books. A library is not a luxury, but one of the necessities of life.
Henry Ward Beecher

Nothing can supply the place of books. They are cheering or soothing companions in solitude, illness, affliction. The wealth of both continents would not compensate for the good they impart. Let every man, if possible, gather some good books under his roof, and obtain access for himself and family to some social library. Almost any luxury should be sacrificed to this.
W. E. Channing

When we are collecting books, we are collecting happiness.
Vincent Starrett

My books! I cannot tell you what they are to me—silent, wealthy, loyal, lovers. I do thank God for my books with every fiber of my being.

Oswald Chambers

I go into my library, and all history unrolls before me. I breathe the morning air of the world while the scent of Eden's roses yet lingered in it, while it vibrated only to the world's first brood of nightingales, and to the laugh of Eve. I see the pyramids building; I heard the shouting of the armies of Alexander.

Alexander Smith

A bookstore is a collection of books, but it is not a library. A library is an organism developing side by side with the mind and character of its owner. It is the house of his spirit and is thus furnished progressively in accordance with the progress of his mental life.

Richard Le Gallienne

A library is true fairyland, a very palace of delight, a haven of repose from the storms and troubles of the world. Rich and poor can enjoy it alike, for here, at least, wealth gives no advantage.

Avebury

Dreams, books, are each a world, and books we know,
Are a substantial world, both pure and good.
Round these, with tendrils strong as flesh and blood,
Our pastime and our happiness will grow.

William Wordsworth

Reading—the nice and subtle happiness of reading … this joy not dulled by age, this polite and unpunished vice, this selfish, serene, lifelong intoxication.

Logan Pearsall Smith

Talk of the happiness of getting a great prize in the lottery! What is that to the opening of a box of books?

Robert Southey

In the highest civilization the book is still the highest delight.

Ralph Waldo Emerson

There is no pleasure so cheap, so innocent, and so remunerative as the real, hearty pleasure and taste for reading.

Robert Lowe

There is something called the rapture of the deep, and it refers to what happens when a deep-sea diver spends too much time at the bottom of the ocean and can't tell which way is up. When he surfaces, he's liable to have a condition called the bends, where the body can't adapt to the oxygen levels in the atmosphere. All of this happens to me when I surface from a great book.

Nora Ephron

The question isn't whether I have time to read or not (time that nobody will ever give me, by the way), but whether I'll allow myself the pleasure of being a reader.

Daniel Pennac

Every reader wants the same thing: to open the cover of a book and watch the words explode like fireworks off the page.

Kim Lehman

Sometimes when Rose was reading, she would catch a whiff of the musty smell of her book.

She put her nose down in the fold and inhaled deeply so that wonderful smell, the smell of adventure in faraway lands, would fill her up. She rubbed her hand across the pages to feel the velvety surface of the paper. When she closed her eyes, her fingertips could even feel the words that were printed there, each letter raised just a little, almost like the special language that her blind aunt Mary could read. To Rose, a book was as real and alive as if it breathed and walked and spoke.

Roger Lea MacBride,
In the Land of the Big Red Apple

People who love reading get an instantly warm feeling in their bellies when they hear others describe getting comfortable with a good book.

Carla H. Krueger

Nothing can supply the place of books. They are cheering or soothing companions in solitude, illness, affliction.

W. E. Channing

3
Children Should Read!

When you put a book in a child's hands, you are bringing that child news of the infinitely varied nature of life. You are an awakener.

Paula Fox

It is the books we read before middle life that do most to mold our characters and influence our lives.

Robert Pitman

There are perhaps no days of our childhood we lived so fully as those we spent with a favorite book.

Marcel Proust

Any book that helps a child to form a habit of reading, to make reading one of his deep and continuing needs, is good for him.

Maya Angelou

Libraries allow children to ask questions about the world and find the answers. And the wonderful thing is that once a child learns to use a library, the doors to learning are always open.

Laura Bush

No book is really worth reading at the age of ten which is not equally (and often far more) worth reading at the age of fifty and beyond.

C. S. Lewis

So it is with children who learn to read fluently and well: They begin to take flight into whole new worlds as effortlessly as young birds take to the sky.

William James

If my life had been more full of calamity than it has been, I would live it over again to have read the books I did in my youth.

William Hazlitt

The books that charmed us in youth recall the

delight ever afterwards; we are hardly persuaded there are any like them, any deserving equally of our affections. Fortunate if the best fall in our way during this susceptible and forming period of our lives.

A. Bronson Alcott

For children, the joy of a book is not merely the story but the feel, the taste, the smell of it—the texture of the paper, the size and shape of the typeface, the illustrations, flaws, marks, even the numbering of the pages.

Pamela Brown

There is a space on everyone's bookshelves for books one has outgrown but cannot give away. They hold one's youth between their leaves, like flowers pressed on a half-forgotten summer's day..

Marion C. Garretty

To learn to read is to light a fire; every syllable that is spelled out is a spark.

Victor Hugo

I learned from the age of two or three that any room in our house, at any time of day, was there to read in, or be read in. My mother read to me. She'd read to me in the big bedroom in the mornings, when we were in her rocker together, which ticked in rhythm as we rocked, as though we had a cricket accompanying the story.

Eudora Welty

I was raised among books, making invisible friends in pages that seemed cast from dust and whose smell I carry on my hands to this day.

Carlos Ruiz Zafon

At one magical instant in your early childhood, the page of a book—that string of confused, alien ciphers—shivered into meaning. Words spoke to you, gave up their secrets; at that moment, whole universes opened. You became, irrevocably, a reader.

Alberto Manguel

There are many little ways to enlarge your child's world. Love of books is the best of all.

Jacqueline Kennedy Onassis

All I have learned, I learned from books.

Abraham Lincoln

There is space on everyone's bookshelves for books you have outgrown but can't give away.

They hold your youth between their pages,
like flowers pressed on a half-forgotten
Summer's day.

Unknown

Blessed are the children of the bookworm for
they shall inherit the books.

Unknown

No book is really worth reading at the age of
ten which is not equally—and often far
more—worth reading at the age of fifty and
beyond.

C. S. Lewis

We shouldn't teach great books; we should
teach a love of reading.

B. F. Skinner

If you want your children to be intelligent,
read them fairy tales. If you want them to be
more intelligent, read them more fairy tales.

Albert Einstein

Once you learn to read, you will be forever
free.

Frederick Douglass

I was raised among books, making invisible

friends in pages that seemed cast from dust and whose smell I carry on my hands to this day.

Carlos Ruiz Zafon

We have an obligation to read aloud to our children. To read them things they enjoy. To read to them stories we are already tired of. To do the voices, to make it interesting, and not to stop reading to them just because they learn to read to themselves. Use reading-aloud time as bonding time, as time when no phones are checked, when the distractions of the world are put aside.

Neil Gaiman

I have this belief that children become readers before they can read. They become hooked on books because they were read aloud to as a child.

Jacqueline Wilson

A child who reads will be an adult who thinks.

Unknown

There's no such thing as a kid who hates reading. There are kids who love reading, and kids who are reading the wrong books.

James Patterson

You're never too old, too wacky, too wild, to pick up a book and read to a child.

Dr. Seuss

I was the kid that was actually excited when the teacher told us to read silently.

Unknown

You're never too young to discover the treasure of a good book!

Amanda R. Browning

A mind needs books as a sword needs a whetstone, if it is to keep its edge.

George R. R. Martin

No book is really worth reading at the age of ten which is not equally (and often far more) worth reading at the age of fifty and beyond.

C. S. Lewis

A child who carries a book with a bookmark in it is in two places at the same time.

Tony Abbott

Children are made readers on the laps of their parents.

Emilie Buchwald

If my life had been more full of calamity than it has been, I would live it over again to have read the books I did in my youth.

William Hazlitt

For children, the joy of a book is not merely the story but the feel, the taste, the smell of it -- the texture of the paper, the size and shape of the typeface, the illustrations, flaws, marks, even the numbering of the pages.

Pamela Brown

It had been startling and disappointing to me to find out that storybooks had been written by people, that books were not natural wonders, coming up of themselves like grass. Yet regardless of where they came from, I cannot remember a time when I was not in love with them—with the books themselves, cover and binding and the paper they were printed on, with their smell and their weight and with their possession in my arms, captured and carried off to myself. Still illiterate, I was ready for them, committed to all the reading I could give them.

Eudora Welty

My early and invincible love of reading ... I

would not exchange for the treasures of India.

Edward Gibbon

In the seemingly endless rainy afternoons I took volume after volume from the shelves. I had always the same certainty of finding a book that was new to me as a man who walks into a field has of finding a new blade of grass.

C. S. Lewis

A truly great book should be read in youth, again in maturity, and once more in old age..

Robertson Davies

Reading books in one's youth is like looking at the moon through a crevice; reading books in middle age is like looking at the moon in one's courtyard; and reading books in old age is like looking at the moon at an open terrace. This is because the depth of benefits of reading varies in proportion to the depth of one's own experience.

Chang Ch'ao

There is no such thing as a child who hates to read; there are only children who have not found the right book.

Frank Serafini

Children should learn that reading is pleasure, not just something that teachers make you do in school.

Beverly Cleary

4
Libraries and Bookstores

Library: the place where you're by
yourself but not alone.

An Unknown Book Lover

Books are delightful society. If you go
into a room and find it full of books—
even without taking them from the
shelves they seem to speak to you, to
bid you welcome.

William Gladstone

A house that has a library
in it has a soul.

Plato

A library is many things. It's a place to go, to get in out of the rain. It's a place to go if you want to sit and think. But particularly it is a place where books live, and where you get in touch with other people, and other thoughts, through books. If you want to find out about something, the information is in the reference books--the dictionaries, the encyclopedias, the atlases. If you like to be told a story, the library is the place to go. Books hold most of the secrets of the world, most of the thoughts that men and women have had. And when you are reading a book, you and the author are alone together—just the two of you.

E. B. White

I never understood people who don't have bookshelves.

George Plimpton

My grandma always said that God made libraries so that people didn't have any excuse to be stupid.

Joan Bauer

I attempted briefly to consecrate myself in the public library, believing every crack in my soul could be chinked with a book.

Barbara Kingsolver

The library is like a candy store where everything is free.

Jamie Ford

Nothing is pleasanter to me than exploring in a library.

Walter Savage Landor

His library was a fine dark place bricked with books, so anything could happen there and always did. All you had to do was pull a book from the shelf and open it and suddenly the darkness was not so dark anymore.

Ray Bradbury

Nothing is more impotent than an unread library.

John Waters

The library would've cheered me up, most days. I loved the heavy oaken tables, the high walls stacked with books to the ceiling, the musty smell of old pages and the heavy brass fixtures that had gone dark with age and wear.

Claudia Gray

Libraries allow children to ask questions about the world and find the answers. And the wonderful thing is that once a child learns to use a library, the doors to learning are always open.

Laura Bush

The library is not, as some would have it, a place for the retiring of disposition or faint of heart. It is not an ivory tower or a quiet room in a sanitarium facing away from the afternoon sun. It is, rather, a command center, a power base. A board room, a war room. An Oval Office for all who preside over their own destinies. One does not retreat from the world here; one prepares to join it at an advantage.

Eric Burns

It may be that I link every library to that first one - to my early childhood experience of drawing on the floor near my father's desk. A library is of course a real place, but it is also an unreal one. What happens there is mostly silent. I think I've always liked the whispering aspect of libraries, the hushing librarians and my feeling of solitude among many.

Siri Hustvedt

You can learn from a glance at anyone's

library, not what they are, but what they wish
to be.

Alan Bradley

History shows that an examination of the
personal collection of titles in any man's
library will provide something of a glimpse
into his soul.

Andrew Smith

Where is the human nature so weak as in the
bookstore?

Henry Ward Beecher

If a book is worth reading, it is worth buying.

John Ruskin

Never lend books, for no one ever returns
them; the only books I have in my library are
books that other folks have lent me.

Anatole France

A home without books is like a room without
windows. A little library, growing every year,
is an honorable part of a man's history. It is a
man's duty to have books. A library is not a
luxury, but one of the necessities of life.

Henry Ward Beecher

Nothing can supply the place of books. They are cheering or soothing companions in solitude, illness, affliction. The wealth of both continents would not compensate for the good they impart. Let every man, if possible, gather some good books under his roof, and obtain access for himself and family to some social library. Almost any luxury should be sacrificed to this.

W. E. Channing

When we are collecting books, we are collecting happiness.

Vincent Starrett

If you go into a room filled with books, even without taking them down from their shelves, they seem to speak to you, to welcome you.

William E. Gladstone

A bookstore is a collection of books, but it is not a library. A library is an organism developing side by side with the mind and character of its owner. It is the house of his spirit and is thus furnished progressively in accordance with the progress of his mental life.

Richard Le Gallienne

A library is true fairyland, a very palace of delight, a haven of repose from the storms and troubles of the world. Rich and poor can enjoy it alike, for here, at least, wealth gives no advantage.

Avebury

A bookstore is one of the only pieces of evidence we have that people are still thinking.

Jerry Seinfield

A bookshelf is as particular to its owner as are his or her clothes; a personality is stamped on a library just as a shoe is shaped by the foot.

Alan Bennett

Book collecting is an obsession, an occupation, a disease, an addiction, a fascination, an absurdity, a fate. It is not a hobby.

Jeanette Winterson

The truly cultured are capable of owning thousands of unread books without losing their composure or their desire for more.

Gabriel Zaid

A library in the middle of a community is a

cross between an emergency exit, a life-raft and a festival. They are cathedrals of the mind; hospitals of the soul; theme parks of the imagination. On a cold rainy island, they are the only sheltered public spaces where you are not consumer, but a citizen instead.

Caitlin Moran

Without libraries, what have we? We have no past and no future.

Ray Bradbury

They say in every library there is a single book that can answer the question that burns like a fire in the mind.

Lemony Snicket

That perfect tranquility of life, which is nowhere to be found but in retreat, a faithful friend and a good library.

Aphra Behn

I do things like get in a taxi and say, "The library, and step on it."

David Foster Wallace

A library is a good place to go when you feel unhappy, for there, in a book, you may find encouragement and comfort. A library is a good place to go when you feel bewildered or undecided, for there, in a book, you may have your question answered. Books are good company, in sad times and happy times, for books are people—people who have managed to stay alive by hiding between the covers of a book.

E. B. White

It isn't just a library. It is a space ship that will take you to the farthest reaches of the universe, a time machine that will take you to the far past and the far future, a teacher that knows more than any human being, a friend that will amuse you and console you—and most of all, a gateway to a better and happier and more useful life.

Isaac Asimov

The feeling of pride you get when you just look at your own bookshelves.

An Unknown Book Lover

Whatever the cost of our libraries, the price is cheap compared to that of an ignorant nation.

Walter Cronkite

What kind of life can you have in a house
without books?

Sherman Alexie

It is a man's duty to have books. A library is
not a luxury, but one of the necessities of life.

Henry Ward Beecher

A library outranks any other one thing a
community can do to benefit its people. It is a
never failing spring in the desert.

Andrew Carnegie

I love walking into a bookstore. It's like all my
friends are sitting on shelves, waving their
pages at me.

Tahereh Mafi

Too many books? I think what you mean is
not enough bookshelves.

An Unknown Book Lover

There's no such thing as too many books.

An Unknown Book Lover

Of course anyone who truly loves books buys
more of them than he or she can hope to read
in one fleeting lifetime. A good book, resting
unopened in its slot on a shelf, full of majestic

potentiality, is the most comforting sort of intellectual wallpaper.

David Quammen

Libraries store the energy that fuels the imagination. They open up windows to the world and inspire us to explore and achieve, and contribute to improving our quality of life. Libraries change lives for the better.

Sidney Sheldon

In a library we are surrounded by many hundreds of dear friends imprisoned by an enchanter in paper and leather boxes.

Ralph Waldo Emerson

She breathed deeply of the scent of decaying fiction, disintegrating history and forgotten verse, and she observed for the first time that a room full of books smelled like dessert: a sweet snack made of figs, vanilla, glue and cleverness.

Joe Hill

A library is a hospital for the mind.

An Unknown Book Lover

Books wrote our life story, as they accumulated on our shelves (and on our windowsills, and underneath our sofa, and on top of our refrigerators), they became chapters in it themselves.

Anne Fadiman

Libraries store the energy that fuels the imagination. They open up windows to the world and inspire us to explore and achieve, and contribute to improving our quality of life. Libraries change lives for the better.

Sidney Sheldon

In a good bookroom you feel in some mysterious way that you are absorbing the wisdom contained in all the books through your skin, without even opening them.

Mark Twain

When trouble strikes, head to the library. You will either be able to solve the problem, or simply have something to read as the world crashes down around you.

Lemony Snickett

I would be most content if my children grow up to be the kind of people who think decorating consists mostly of building enough bookshelves.

Anna Quindlen

To build up a library is to create life. It's never just a random collection of books.

Carlos Maria Dominguez

The library is the temple of learning and learning has liberated more people than all the wars in history.

Carl T. Rowan

A little library, growing larger every year, is an honorable part of a man's history. It is a man's duty to have books. A library is not a luxury, but one of the necessities of life.

Henry Ward Beecher

I don't have to look far to find treasures. I discover them every time I visit a library.

Michael Embry

What is a bookshelf other than a treasure chest for a curious mind.

An Unknown Book Lover

If I saved all the money I spent on books, I'd spend it on books.

An Unknown Book Lover

A library in the middle of a community is a cross between an emergency exit, a life-raft and a festival. They are cathedrals of the mind; hospitals of the soul; theme parks of the imagination. On a cold rainy island, they are the only sheltered public spaces where you are not a consumer, but a citizen instead.

Caitlen Moran

I'm the kind of girl who fantasizes about being trapped in a library overnight.

Fangirl Rainbow Rowell

I stepped into the bookshop and breathed in that perfume of paper and magic that strangely no one had ever thought of bottling.

Carlos Ruiz Zafon

I love walking into a bookstore. It's like all my friends are sitting on shelves, waving their pages at me.

Tahereh Mafi

Congratulations on the new library, because it isn't just a library. It is a space ship that will take you to the farthest reaches of the Universe, a time machine that will take you to the far past and the far future, a teacher that knows more than any human being, a friend that will amuse you and console you--and most of all, a gateway, to a better and happier and more useful life.

Isaac Asimov

For an impoverished child whose family could not afford to buy books, the library was the open door to wonder and achievement, and I can never be sufficiently grateful that I had the wit to charge through that door and make the most of it. Now, when I read constantly about the way in which library funds are being cut and cut, I can only think that the door is closing and that American society has found one more way to destroy itself.

Isaac Asimov

I would desire to have no other prison than a library, and to be chained together with as many good authors.

Robert Burton

Libraries are the wardrobes of literature.

George Dyer

I go into my library, and all history unrolls before me.

Alexander Smith

Libraries raised me.

Ray Bradbury

A bookshelf is as particular to its owner as are his or her clothes; a personality is stamped on a library just as a shoe is shaped by the foot.

Alan Bennett

They say in every library there is a single book that can answer the question that burns like a fire in the mind.

Lemony Snicket

That perfect tranquility of life, which is nowhere to be found but in retreat, a faithful friend and a good library.

Aphra Behn

A library is a good place to go when you feel unhappy, for there, in a book, you may find encouragement and comfort. A library is a good place to go when you feel bewildered or undecided, for there, in a book, you may have your question answered. Books are good company, in sad times and happy times, for books are people—people who have managed to stay alive by hiding between the covers of a book.

E. B. White

The feeling of pride you get when you just look at your own bookshelves.

An Unknown Book Lover

What kind of life can you have in a house without books.

Sherman Alexie

Whatever the cost of our libraries, the price is cheap compared to that of an ignorant nation.

Walter Cronkite

It is a man's duty to have books. A library is not a luxury, but one of the necessities of life.

Henry Ward Beecher

A library outranks any other one thing a community can do to benefit its people. It is a never failing spring in the desert.

Andrew Carnegie

5
The Habit of Reading

If you read just 15 minutes a day,
in one year you will have read over
1,000,000 words.

Source: Statisticbrain.com

To acquire the habit of reading is to
construct for yourself a refuge from
almost all the miseries of life.

W. Somerset Maugham

Keep reading.
It's one of the most marvelous
adventures that anyone can have.

Lloyd Alexander

Read. Everything you can get your hands on. Read until words become your friends. Then when you need to find one, they will jump into your mind, waving their hands for you to pick them. And you can select whichever you like, just like a captain choosing a stickball team.

Karen Witemeyer

Often I sat up in my room reading the greatest part of the night, when the book was borrowed in the evening and to be returned early in the morning, lest it should be missed or wanted.

Benjamin Franklin

Make wise choices about what you read. Read only what is necessary or worthwhile. And then take the time to read carefully. One book read with concentration and reflected upon is worth a hundred flashed through without any absorption at all.

Eknath Easwaran

The way a book is read—which is to say, the qualities a reader brings to a book—can have as much to do with its worth as anything the author puts into it … Anyone who can read can learn how to read deeply and thus live more fully.

Norman Cousins

Every man who knows how to read has it in his power to magnify himself, to multiply the ways in which he exists, to make his life full, significant and interesting.

Aldous Huxley

In a very real sense, people who have read good literature have lived more than people who cannot or will not read. . . . It is not true that we can have only one life to live; if we can read, we can live as many more lives and as many kinds of lives as we wish.

S. I. Hayakawa

Reading books in one's youth is like looking at the moon through a crevice; reading books in middle age is like looking at the moon in one's courtyard; and reading books in old age is like looking at the moon at an open terrace. This is because the depth of benefits of reading varies in proportion to the depth of one's own experience.

Chang Ch'ao

Of all the inanimate objects, of all men's creations, books are the nearest to us, for they contain our very thoughts, our ambitions, our indignations, our illusions, our fidelity to truth, and our persistent leaning toward error. But most of all they resemble us in the precarious hold on life.

Joseph Conrad

Reading is to the mind what exercise is to the body.

Joseph Addison

He that loves reading has everything within his reach.

William Godwin

Reading—the nice and subtle happiness of reading…This joy not dulled by age, this polite and unpunished vice, this selfish, serene, lifelong intoxication.

Logan Pearsall Smith

Some day you will be old enough to start reading fairy tales again.

C. S. Lewis

Reading fiction is important. It is a vital means of imagining a life other than your own, which in turn makes us more empathetic beings. Following complex story lives stretches our brains beyond the 140 characters of sound-bite thinking, and staying within the world of a novel gives us the ability to be quiet and alone, two skills that are disappearing faster than the polar icecaps.

Ann Patchett

Reading is the life-saving water for our minds. Drink pure words as much as you need and remain alive.

Munia Khan

The world belongs to those who read.

Rick Holland

A book problem: you don't mind waiting, because it gives you an excuse to read.

Unknown

There's nothing wrong with reading a book you love over and over. When you do, the words get inside you, become a part of you, in a way that words in a book you've only read once can't.

Gail Carson Levine

There are too many books that one must read

in a lifetime to ever be bored.

Nicholas Erickson

I try to carry books with me wherever I go. Their weight has become like ballast against the churning sea of modern life, where so many real things are vanishing, and so many beautiful things are being made invisible.

Unknown

It's always better to have too much to read than not enough.

Ann Patchett

Between the pages of a book is a lovely place to be.

An Unknown Book Lover

Reading makes you to be quiet in a world that no longer makes place for that.

John Green

A day without reading is like ... Just kidding. I have no idea.

An Unknown Book Lover

A reader lives a thousand lives before he dies. The man who never reads lives only one.

George R. R Martin

I like books that aren't just lovely but that have memories in themselves. Just like playing a song, picking up a book again that has memories can take you back to another place or another time.

Emma Watson

It is what you read when you don't have to that determines what you will be when you can't help it.

Oscar Wilde

Books are the perfect entertainment: no commercials, no batteries, hours of enjoyment for each dollar spent. What I wonder if why everybody doesn't carry a book around for those inevitable dead spots in life.

Stephen King

It is most likely that I will die next to a pile of books I was meaning to read.

Lemony Snicket

I woke up thinking a very pleasant thought: there is lots left in the world to read.

Nicholson Baker

If one cannot enjoy reading a book over and

over again there is no use reading it at all.

Oscar Wilde

I find television very educating. Every time somebody turns on the set, I go into the other room and read a book.

Groucho Marx

I can't imagine someone really enjoying a book and reading it only once.

C. S. Lewis

I read a book one day and my whole life was changed.

Orhan Pamuk

Surprising what you can dig out of books if you read long enough, isn't it.

Robert Jordan

Of all the diversions of life, there is none so proper to fill up its empty spaces as the reading of useful and entertaining authors.

Joseph Addison

I keep a book or two in my car, often getting in a quick paragraph at a stoplight. If you happen to be behind me, please don't honk when the light turns green, for I could be coming to the end of a paragraph.

Joseph Epstein

Read few books well.

John Horne Tooke

More is got from one book on which the thought settles for a definite end in knowledge, than from libraries skimmed over by a wandering eye.

Edward Bulwer-Lytton

Some books are to be tasted, others to be swallowed, and some few to be chewed and digested.

Francis Bacon

Read. Read until your eyes are sore. Then read some more.

Lisa Bloom

Lost in a book is a great place to be found.

Shannon Taylor Hodnett

Never trust anyone who has not brought a book with them.

Lemony Snicket

I love the solitude of reading. I love the deep

dive into someone else's story, the delicious ache of a last page.

Naomi Shihab Nye

There were a lot of things I planned to do. Then I picked up a book.

An Unknown Book Lover

The habit of reading is the only enjoyment I know in which there is no alloy. It lasts when all other pleasures fade. It will be there to support you when all other resources are gone. It will be present to you when the energies of your body have fallen away from you. It will last you until your death. It will make your hours pleasant to you as long as you live.

Anthony Trollope

6

The Glorious Addiction of Reading

Abibliophobia:
(Un-bib-li-uh-fo-bee-uh)
The fear of running out
of reading material

True book addicts sneeze with their eyes
open so they don't miss a word.

An Unknown Book Lover

I am simply a book drunkard.

L. M. Montgomery

I keep a book or two in my car, often getting in a quick paragraph at a stoplight. If you happen to be behind me, please don't honk when the light turns green, for I could be coming to the end of a paragraph.

Joseph Epstein

When I get a little money, I buy books. If any is left, I buy food and clothes.

Erasmus

The cure for boredom is books. There is no cure for books.

Unknown

Literature duplicates the experience of living in a way that nothing else can, drawing you so fully into another life that you temporarily forget you have one of your own. That is why you read it, and might even sit up in bed 'til early dawn, throwing your whole tomorrow out of whack, simply to find out what happens to some people who, you know perfectly well, are made up.

Barbara Kingsolver

A good book is all-consuming: part of it becomes you, and part of you becomes it.

Wisława Szymborska

Owning an e-reader does not mean that I don't appreciate my books. It means that I can't stand to be without them.

Unknown

We are, as a species, addicted to story. Even when the body goes to sleep, the mind stays up all night, telling itself stories.

Jonathan Gottschall

I hate it when an awesome book isn't part of a series, and you don't get to read any more.

Unknown

Book collecting is an obsession, an occupation, a disease, an addiction, a fascination, an absurdity, a fate. It is not a hobby.

Jeanette Winterson

I do not want to just read books. I want to climb inside them and live there.

Unknown

If the crowns of all the kingdoms of Europe

were laid down at my feet in exchange for my books and my love of reading, I would spurn them all.

Francois Fenelon

The odd thing about people that have lots of books is that they always want more.

Unknown

I always read. You know how sharks have to keep swimming or they die? I'm like that. If I stop reading, I die.

Patrick Rothfuss

Bookworms will rule the world. As soon as we finish one more chapter.

Unknown

Books to the ceiling,
Books to the sky,
My pile of books is a mile high.
How I love them! How I need them!
I've have a long beard by the time I read them.

Arnold Lobel

All good books must come to an end.
Sigh...

An Unknown Book Lover

I cannot imagine life without books any more than I can imagine life without breathing.

Terry Brooks

Why can't I just read all day, every day.

Unknown

Wear the old coat and buy the new book.

Austin Phelps

I read my eyes out and can't read half enough ... the more one reads the more one sees we have to read.

John Adams

At times I think to myself, "Drop the book and get stuff done. Then, I laugh and turn the page.

Unknown

I tried everything to get to sleep last night. Well, everything except closing the book and putting it on the nightstand. Let's not get too crazy.

Unknown

You cannot pretend to read a book. Your eyes will give you away. So will your breathing. A person entranced by a book simply forgets to breathe. The house can catch alight and a reader deep in a book will not look up until the wallpaper is in flames.

Lloyd Jones

I must have books everywhere. They're the soul of a room--they reveal the taste, the interests, and the secrets of whoever lives there.

Diane von Furstenberg

When I get a little money, I buy books; and if any is left, I buy food and clothes.

Desiderius Erasmus

The thing about books was, the more you read and liked them, the more you wanted to have on hand to read. Before you knew it you needed more bookshelves, and then all of the sudden they filled your house.

Sui Ishida

Of course anyone who truly loves books buys more of them than he or she can hope to read in one fleeting lifetime. A good book, resting unopened in its slot on a shelf, full of majestic potentiality, is the most comforting sort of intellectual wallpaper.

David Quammen

7
The Comfort of Reading

I've never known any trouble that an hour's reading didn't assuage.

Charles de Secondat

Just the knowledge that a good book is waiting one at the end of a long day makes that day happier.

Kathleen Norris

Sometimes a book is the only thing that can make the world right again.

Unknown

There is a wonder in reading Braille that the sighted will never know: to touch words and have them touch you back.

Jim Fiebig

It is from books that wise men derive consolation in the troubles of life.

Victor Hugo

They are for company the best friends, in doubts counselors, in damps comforters, time's perspective, the home-traveler's ship or horse, the busy man's best recreation, the opiate of idle weariness, the mind's best ordinary, nature's garden, and the seed-plot of immortality.

Bulstrode Whitelocke

The familiar faces of my books welcomed me. I threw myself into my reading chair and gazed around me with pleasure. All my old friends present—there in spirit, ready to talk with me, any moment when I was in the mood, making no claim upon my attention when I was not.

George MacDonald

In the seemingly endless rainy afternoons I took volume after volume from the shelves. I had always the same certainty of finding a book that was new to me as a man who walks into a field has of finding a new blade of grass.

C. S. Lewis

Books become as familiar and necessary as old friends. Each change in them, brought about by much handling and by accident only endears them more. They are an extension of oneself.

Charlotte Gray

The first time I read an excellent book, it is to me just as if I had gained a new friend. When I read over a book I have perused before, it resembles the meeting with an old one.

Oliver Goldsmith

Books are delightful when prosperity happily smiles; when adversity threatens, they are inseparable comforters. They give strength to human compacts, nor are grave opinions brought forward without books. Arts and sciences, the benefits of which no mind can calculate, depend on book.

Richard De Bury

When I am reading a book, whether wise or

silly, it seems to me to be alive and talking to me.

Jonathan Swift

Friends, books, a cheerful heart, and
conscience clear,
Are the most choice companions we have
here

William Mather

Oh! but books are such safe company! They
keep your Secrets well; they never boast they
made your eyes glisten, or your cheek flush, or
your heart throb. You may take up your
favorite Author, and love him at a distance
just as warmly as you like, for all the sweet
fancies and glowing thoughts that have
winged your lonely hours so fleetly and so
sweetly. Then you may close the book, and
lean your cheek against the cover, as if it were
the face of a dear friend; shut your eyes and
soliloquize to your heart's content, without
fear of misconstruction ... You may put the
volume under your pillow, and let your eye
and the first ray of morning light fall on it
together, and nothing shall rob you of that
delicious pleasure. You may have a thousand
petty, provoking, irritating annoyances

through the day, and you shall come back to your dear old book, and forget them all in dreamland. It shall be a friend that shall be always at hand; that shall never try you by caprice, or pain you by forgetfulness, or wound you by distrust.

Sara P. Parton

Books—you are wonderful. In you live the hope, the comfort, the philosophy, the glory, the peace, the reward of a world. You line the edge of my life. As I view you—of a thousand lives expressed and of a hundred thousand thoughts revealed—I say that come what may, so long as I stick to you, I shall not be entirely alone.

George Matthew Adams

Books are the quietest and most constant friends; they are the most accessible and wisest of counselors, and the most patient of teachers.

Charles W. Eliot

Except a living man there is nothing more wonderful than a book! –a message to us from the dead—from human souls we never saw, and who lived perhaps thousands of miles away; and yet these words on those little sheets of paper speak to us, amuse us, and comfort us.

Charles Kingsley

The peace of great books be for you,
Stains of pressed clover leaves on pages,
Bleach of the light of years held in leather.

Carl Sandburg

I hope that ... they did for you what any good story should do—make you forget the real stuff weighing on your mind for a little while and take you away to a place you've never been.

Stephen King

I have sought repose everywhere, and I have found it only in a little corner with a little book.

St. Francois de Sales

Some days getting lost in a book is by far the best option.

An Unknown Book Lover

Sometimes I think getting lost in my books is better than living my own life. I just want to be someone else for a few hours.

An Unknown Book Lover

I have a shelf of comfort books, which I read when the world closes in on me or something untoward happens.

Anne McCaffrey

I found comfort through literature. I loved getting lost in things as marvelous and as wonderful as books. They made me forget about my own troubles; like a submarine and the sea, they submerged me so perfectly.

An Unknown Book Lover

Let's get lost in a world made of books, coffee and rainy days.

An Unknown Book Lover

Many people, myself among them, feel better at the mere sight of a book.

Jane Smiley

Book love is something like romantic love. When we are reading a really great book, burdens feel lighter, cares seem smaller.

Steve Leveen

I see a book, I see a coffee, I see a good day ahead.

An Unknown Book Lover

The secret to a well-balanced life is a cup of
tea in one hand and a book in the other.
An Unknown Book Lover

I lived in books more than I lived anywhere
else.
Neil Gaiman

My soul found ease and rest in the
companionship of books.
Pat Conroy

Just the knowledge that a good book is
awaiting one at the end of a long day makes
that day happier.
Kathleen Norris

In the winter she curls up around a good
book and dreams away the cold.
Ben Aaronovitch

Books have been my classroom and my
confidant. Books have widened my horizons.
Books have comforted me in my hardest
times. Books have changed my life.
Po Bronson

That's how it is with books, isn't it: they're
not in a hurry. They'll wait for you till you're

ready. People empty me. I have to go away to refill.

Charles Bukowski

Many people, myself among them, feel better at the mere sight of a book.

Jane Smiley

Here's to books, the cheapest vacation you can buy.

Charlaine Harris

To sit alone in the lamplight with a book spread out before you, and hold intimate converse with men of unseen generations— such is a pleasure beyond compare.

Kenko Yoshida

Reading gives us someplace to go when we have to stay where we are.

Mason Cooley

Books let you fight dragons, meet the love of your life, travel to faraway lands and laugh alongside friends, all within their pages. They're an escape that brings you home.

Unknown

I found comfort through literature. I loved

getting lost in things as marvelous and as wonderful as books. They made me forget about my own troubles, like a submarine and the sea, they submerged me so perfectly.

An Unknown Book Lover

Happiness is soft pajamas and a good book, and time enough to indulge in both.

An Unknown Book Lover

Reading and eating are two pleasures that combine admirably.

C. S. Lewis

It was books that made me feel that perhaps I was not completely alone.

Cassandra Clare

Book love is something like romantic love. When we are reading a really great book, burdens feel lighter, cares seem smaller.

Steve Leveen

An extrovert looks at a stack of books and see a stack of papers, while an introvert looks at the same stack and sees a soothing source of escape.

Eric Samuel Timm

Books are the quietest and most constant of friends; they are the most accessible and wisest of counselors, and the most patient of teachers.

Charles William Eliot

Some books are so familiar that reading them is like being home again.

Louisa May Alcott

The best moments in reading are when you come across something—a thought, a feeling, a way of looking at things—that you'd thought special, particular to you. And here it is, set down by someone else, a person you've never met, maybe even someone long dead. And it's as if a hand has come out, and taken yours.

Alan Bennett

We don't need to have just one favorite. We keep adding favorites. Our favorite book is always the book that speaks most directly to us at a particular stage in our lives. And our lives change. We have other favorites that give us what we most need at that particular time. But we never lose the old favorites. They're always with us. We just sort of accumulate them.

Lloyd Alexander

Here's to fresh coffee and good books and kind hearts and found beauty and the weird, kindred souls who help us know that we're all in this together.

Nanea Hoffman

I love books. I love that moment when you open one and sink into it. You can escape from the world, into a story that's way more interesting than yours will ever be.

Elizabeth Scott

Reading a good book in silence is like eating chocolate for the rest of your life and never getting fat.

Becca Fitzpatrick

Oh, I just want what we all want: a comfortable couch, a nice beverage, a weekend of no distractions and a book that will stop time, lift me out of my quotidian existence and alter my thinking forever.

Elizabeth Gilbert

It is from books that wise men derive

consolation in the troubles of life.

Victor Hugo

They are for company the best friends, in doubts counselors, in damps comforters, time's perspective, the home-traveler's ship or horse, the busy man's best recreation, the opiate of idle weariness, the mind's best ordinary, nature's garden, and the seed-plot of immortality.

Bulstrode Whitelocke

Just the knowledge that a good book is waiting one at the end of a long day makes that day happier.

Kathleen Norris

The love of reading enables a man to exchange the wearisome hours of life, which come to everyone, for hours of delight.

Montesquieu

Books are delightful when prosperity happily smiles; when adversity threatens, they are inseparable comforters. They give strength to human compacts, nor are grave opinions brought forward without books. Arts and sciences, the benefits of which no mind can calculate, depend on books.

Richard De Bury

It is a sign of intimacy to be able to read in the same room with another person, as trusting as dreaming with someone right beside you.

Laura Furman/Elinore Standard

I hope that ... they did for you what any good story should do—make you forget the real stuff weighing on your mind for a little while and take you away to a place you've never been.

Stephen King

Books—you are wonderful. In you live the hope, the comfort, the philosophy, the glory, the peace, the reward of a world. You line the edge of my life. As I view you—of a thousand lives expressed and of a hundred thousand thoughts revealed—I say that come what may, so long as I stick to you, I shall not be entirely alone.

George Matthew Adams

That is part of the beauty of all literature. You discover that your longings are universal longings, that you're not alone and isolated from anyone. You belong.

F. Scott Fitzgerald

The peace of great books be for you,
Stains of pressed clover leaves on pages,
Bleach of the light of years held in leather.

Carl Sandburg

Sometimes a book is the only thing that can
make the world right again.

An Unknown Book Lover

Maybe this is why we read, and why in
moments of darkness we return to books: to
find words for what we already know.

Alberto Manguel

The most comfortable place for a tired mind
is in the lap of a book.

Aman Jassal

Only a true reader will understand how lovely
it is to read a book on rainy days.

Nicholas Spencer

Writing and reading decrease our sense of
isolation. It's like singing on a boat during a
terrible storm at sea. You can't stop the raging
storm, but singing can change the hearts and

spirits of the people who are together on that ship.

Anne Lamott

Some days getting lost in a book is by far the best option.

An Unknown Book Lover

I have a shelf of comfort books, which I read when the world closes in on me or something untoward happens.

Anne McCaffrey

I found comfort through literature. I loved getting lost in things as marvelous and as wonderful as books. They made me forget about my own troubles; like a submarine and the sea, they submerged me so perfectly.

An Unknown Book Lover

Let's get lost in a world made of books, coffee and rainy days.

An Unknown Book Lover

8
Reading in Bed

Physically I'm tired at the end
of the day and quite glad to be reading
in bed by midnight.

Bob Geldof

I go to bed early and rise late and feel as
if I have hardly slept, probably because I
have been reading the entire time.

Daniel Handler

To read in bed is to draw around us invisible, noiseless curtains. Then at last we are in a room of our own and are ready to burrow back, back to that private life of the imagination we all led as a child and to whose secret satisfactions so many of us have mislaid the key.

Clifton Fadiman

Only one hour in the normal day is more pleasurable than the hour spent in bed with a book before going to sleep, and that is the hour spent in bed with a book after being called in the morning.

Rose Macauley

Librocubicularist
(lib-ro-kyoo-bi-kyoo-la-rist)
A person who reads in bed

Book lovers never go to bed alone.

An Unknown Book Lover

If only books were printed with glow in the dark ink. Life would be so much easier.

An Unknown Book Lover

By now, it is probably very late at night, and you have stayed up to read this book when you should have gone to sleep. If this is the case, then I commend you for falling into my trap. It is a writer's greatest pleasure to hear that someone was kept up until the unholy hours of the morning reading one of his books. It goes back to authors being terrible people who delight in the suffering of others. Plus, we get a kickback from the caffeine industry.

Brandon Sanderson

Woke up this morning with a terrific urge to lie in bed all day and read.

Raymond Carver

All good and true book-lovers practice the pleasing and improving avocation of reading in bed … No book can be appreciated until it has been slept with and dreamed over.

Eugene Field

I have always loved reading. Ever since I was a young girl I had a book by my bed and would get lost in the world of make believe.

Lauren Conrad

You know it's a good book when, whilst reading in bed, you'd rather risk drifting off and dropping a book on your face, than wait until later to finish the chapter.

Mary Layton

To Anthony life was a struggle against death, that waited at every corner. It was a concession to his hypochondriacal imagination that he formed the habit of reading in bed—it soothed him. He read until he was tired and often fell asleep with the lights on.

F. Scott Fitzgerald

Only one hour in the normal day is more pleasurable than the hour spent in bed with a book before going to sleep, and that is the hour spent in bed with a book after being called in the morning.

Rose Macauley

Often I sat up in my room reading the greatest part of the night, when the book was borrowed in the evening and to be returned early in the morning, lest it should be missed or wanted.

Benjamin Franklin

Every morning I tell myself, "I'll sleep early

tonight." And every night I say, "One more chapter."

Joyce Rachelle

Literature duplicates the experience of living in a way that nothing else can, drawing you so fully into another life that you temporarily forget you have one of your own. That is why you read it, and might even sit up in bed 'til early dawn, throwing your whole tomorrow out of whack, simply to find out what happens to some people who, you know perfectly well, are made up.

Barbara Kingsolver

We read in bed because reading is halfway between life and dreaming, our own consciousness in someone else's mind.

Anna Quindlen

Knowing you have something good to read before bed is among the most pleasurable of sensations.

Vladimir Nabokov

Bed is the best place for reading, thinking or doing nothing.

Doris Lessing

9
Reading Just For The Fun Of It

If you read one book a week, starting at the age of 5, and live to be 80, you will have read a grand total of 3,900 books, a little over one-tenth of one percent of the books currently in print.

Lewis Buzbee

Let's be reasonable and add an eighth day to the week that is devoted exclusively to reading.

Lena Dunham

In case of good books the point is not to see how many of them you can get through, but rather how many can get through to you.

Mortimer Jerome Adler

Books allow me to get lost in the right direction.

Terry Leibel

Life is a book, and there are a thousand pages I have not yet read.

Will Herondale

A good book is all-consuming: part of it becomes you, and part of you becomes it.

Wisława Szymborska

There is a great deal of difference between the eager man who wants to read a book, and the tired man who wants a book to read.

George MacDonald

My best friend is a person who will give me a book I have not read.

Abraham Lincoln

That is part of the beauty of all literature. You discover that your longings are universal longings, that you're not alone and isolated from anyone. You belong.

F. Scott Fitzgerald

The collaboration between the book and the reader is intimate, private. We must not forget that pleasure, discretion, silence, and creative solitude are the primary characteristics of a life of reading, its most tangible justification and most immediate reward. Solitude may appear now to be an unaffordable luxury, yet any book creates for the reader a place elsewhere. A person reading is a person suspended between the immediate and the timeless. This suspension serves a purpose that has little to do with escaping from the real world, the sin avid readers are most commonly accused of.

Vartan Gregorian

There were a lot of things I planned to do. Then I picked up a book.

Unknown

Never judge a book by its movie.

J. W. Eagan

If you read one book a week, starting at the age of 5, and live to be 80, you will have read a grand total of 3,900 books, a little over one-tenth of one percent of the books currently in print.

Lewis Buzbee

Books have been my classroom and my confidant. Books have widened my horizons. Books have comforted me in my hardest times. Books have changed my life.

Po Bronson

When you read a line that is so well-written, you just close the book and stare at the wall for a minute.

Unknown

Read the best books first, or you may not have a chance to read them at all.

Henry David Thoreau

Good books don't give up all their secrets at once.

Stephen King

In the end, we'll all become stories.

Margaret Atwood

No two persons ever read the same book.

Edmund Wilson

Why can't people just sit and read books and be nice to each other.

David Baldacci

When I'm really into a novel, I'm seeing the world differently at that time. Not just for the hour or so in the day when I get to read. I'm actually walking around in a bit of a haze, spellbound by the book and looking at everything through a different prism.

Colin Firth

You can never get a cup of tea large enough or a book long enough to suit me.

C. S. Lewis

He said: "Books or me." I sometimes remember him when I'm buying new books.

An Unknown Book Lover

When I am reading a book, whether wise or silly, it seems to me to be alive and talking to me.

Jonathan Swift

We use books like mirrors, gazing into them only to discover ourselves.

Joseph Epstein

How many a man has dated a new era in his life from the reading of a book!

Henry David Thoreau

The collaboration between the book and the reader is intimate, private. We must not forget that pleasure, discretion, silence, and creative solitude are the primary characteristics of a life of reading, its most tangible justification and most immediate reward. Solitude may appear now to be an unaffordable luxury, yet any book creates for the reader a place elsewhere. A person reading is a person suspended between the immediate and the timeless. This suspension serves a purpose that has little to do with escaping from the real world, the sin avid readers are most commonly accused of.

Vartan Gregorian

Books may preach when the author cannot, when the author may not, when the author dares not, yea, and which is more, when the author is not.

Thomas Brooks

Life is too short to read books that I'm not enjoying.

Melissa Marr

Judge a book by the way you feel after you read the last page.

B. B. Free

I guess you can call me "old fashioned." I prefer the book with the pages that you can actually turn. Sure, I may have to lick the tip of my fingers so that the pages don't stick together when I'm enraptured in a story that I can't wait to get to the next page. But nothing beats the sound that an actual, physical book makes when you first crack it open or the smell of new, fresh printed words on the creamy white paper of a page turner.

Felicia Johnson

The cure for boredom is books. There is no cure for books.

Unknown

For me, books have always been the greatest gifts. I love to give and receive them because I know they are a reflection of the giver.

Colleen Mariotti

People who say they don't have time to read simply don't want to.

Julie Rugg

To sit alone in the lamplight with a book
spread out before you, and hold intimate
converse with men of unseen generations—
such is a pleasure beyond compare.

Kenko Yoshida

Owning an e-reader does not mean that I
don't appreciate my books. It means that I
can't stand to be without them.

An Unknown Book Lover

Idea:

When your friends ask you what you want for your birthday, tell them to give you *their* favorite book.

Idea:

Add "Read books" to your to-do list every day so you will get at least one thing done.

Idea:

Make a T-shirt which reads,
"I'd rather be reading."

10
The Friendship of Books

Books are the quietest and most
constant friends; they are the most
accessible and wisest of counsellors, and
the most patient of teachers.

Charles W. Eliot

It is the friendship of books that has
made me perfectly happy.

Attributed to Erasmus

The familiar faces of my books welcomed me. I threw myself into my reading chair and gazed around me with pleasure. All my old friends present—there in spirit, ready to talk with me, any moment when I was in the mood, making no claim upon my attention when I was not.

George MacDonald

If you cannot read all your books, at any rate handle, or as it were, fondle them—peer into them, let them fall open where they will, read from the first sentence that arrests the eye, set them back on the shelves with your own hands, arrange them on your own plan so that you at least know where they are. Let them be your friends; let them at any rate be your acquaintances.

Winston Churchill

Books become as familiar and necessary as old friends. Each change in them, brought about by much handling and by accident only endears them more. They are an extension of oneself.

Charlotte Gray

The first time I read an excellent book, it is to me just as if I had gained a new friend. When

I read over a book I have perused before, it resembles the meeting with an old one.

Oliver Goldsmith

Friends, books, a cheerful heart, and conscience clear,
Are the most choice companions we have here.

William Mather

Oh! but books are such safe company! They keep your Secrets well; they never boast they made your eyes glisten, or your cheek flush, or your heart throb. You may take up your favorite author, and love him at a distance just as warmly as you like, for all the sweet fancies and glowing thoughts that have winged your lonely hours so fleetly and so sweetly. Then you may close the book, and lean your cheek against the cover, as if it were the face of a dear friend; shut your eyes and soliloquize to your heart's content, without fear of misconstruction … You may put the volume under your pillow, and let your eye and the first ray of morning light fall on it together, and nothing shall rob you of that delicious pleasure. You may have a thousand petty, provoking, irritating annoyances through the day, and you shall come back to your dear old book, and forget them all in dreamland. It shall be a friend that shall be always at hand; that shall never try you by caprice, or pain you by forgetfulness, or wound you by distrust.

Sara P. Parton

A blessed companion is a book—a book that, fitly chosen, is a lifelong friend.

Douglas Jerrod

Books are our best friends, guiders and philosophers. Books uphold and encourage us when we feel sad and despondent. They bring light into darkness and the sunshine into shadow.

Charmin Patel

Books help my mind soar. They even feel like friends when the real ones let you down.

An Unknown Book Lover

You have but to read with feeling and the book will become a living person to you.

Temple Scott

Whoever acknowledges himself to be a zealous follower of truth, of happiness, of wisdom, of science, or even of the faith, must

of necessity make himself a Lover of Books.
Richard De Bury

When I am reading a book, whether wise or silly, it seems to be alive and talking to me.
Jonathan Swift

In turning to a well-known author, there is not only an assurance that my time will not be thrown away, or my palate nauseated with the most insipid or vilest trash, --but I shake hands with, and look at an old, tried and valued friend in the face,--and compare notes and chat the hours away.
William Hazlitt

Good books, like good friends, are few and chosen; the more select the more enjoyable.
A. Bronson Alcott

My favorite books have a personality and complexion as distinctly drawn as if the author's portrait were framed into the paragraphs and smiled upon me as I read his illustrated pages. Nor could I spare them from my table or shelves, though I should not open the leaves for a twelve-month;--the sight of them, the knowledge that they are within reach, accessible at any moment, rewards me when I invite their company.

A. Bronson Alcott

Books themselves, after long companionship, come to have an actual personality for many of us.

Blackwood's Magazine:
The Companionship of Books

Just as one can sit in silence with an old and intimate friend, or walk by his side with a quiet satisfaction, without caring to be continually chattering, and the feeling of companionship is none the less real because each is pursuing at the moment his own separate line of thought—so it is with some of the occupants of my study-shelves.

Blackwood's Magazine:
The Companionship of Books

Oh! But books are such safe company! They keep your secrets well; they never boast that they made your eyes glisten, or your cheeks flush, or your heart throb. You may take up your favorite author, and love him at a distance just as warmly as you like, for all the sweet fancies and glowing thoughts that have winged your lonely hours so fleetly and so sweetly. Then you may close the book, and learn your cheek against the cover, as if it were the face of a dear friend.

Sara P. Parton

Silent companions of the lonely hour,
Friends, who can never alter or forsake…

Mrs. C. Norton

How vast the debt to books we owe.
Yes! Friends they are! And friends thro' life to last!

John Kenyon

I think we should all of us be grateful for books; they are our best friends and most faithful companions. They instruct, cheer, elevate, and ennoble us; and in whatever mood we go to them, they never frown upon us, but receive us with cordial and loving sincerity.

George Searle Phillips

Books are the windows through which the soul looks out.

Henry Ward Beecher

If you go into a room filled with books, and even without taking them down from their shelves, they seem to speak to you, seem to welcome you, seem to tell you that they have something inside their covers that will be good for you, and that they are willing and desirous to impart it to you.

W. E. Gladstone

We should choose our books as we would our companions, for their sterling and intrinsic merit.

Charles Caleb Colton

You may have a thousand petty, provoking, irritating annoyances through the day, and you shall come back again to your dear old book, and forget them all in dreamland. It shall be a friend that shall always be at hand.

Sara P. Parton

A book can be a great friend, an advisor, a means to an end. A book reveals so much more than a movie would ever do. For example, when I watched the movie "The Hours" I was fascinated by the story. Just a year later I decided to read the book. And what was my surprise that I was even more dazzled by its writings than I was by the images... The images in my head were more vivid than the film could ever transport me to that feminine universe that the author was trying (and so successfully granted me) to conceive...

Ana Claudia Antunes

Take some books and read; that's an immense help; and books are always good company if you have the right sort."

Louisa May Alcott

Books are keys to wisdom's treasure;
Books are paths that upward lead;
Books are gates to lands of pleasure
Books are friends,
Come, let us read.

An Unknown Book Lover

I love walking into a bookstore. It's like all my friends are sitting on shelves, waving their pages at me.

Tahereh Mafi

11
Miscellaneous Thoughts

Talk of the happiness of getting a great prize in the lottery! What is that to the opening of a box of books!

Robert Southey

A well-composed book is a magic carpet on which we are wafted to a world that we cannot enter in any other way.

Caroline Gordon

Books are many things: lullabies for the weary, ointment for the wounded, armor for the fearful and nests for those in need of a home.

Glenda Millard

A well-composed book is a magic carpet on which we are wafted to a world that we cannot enter in any other way.

Caroline Gordon

Of all the diversions of life, there is none so proper to fill up its empty spaces as the reading of useful and entertaining authors.

Joseph Addison

A classic is a book that has never finished saying what it has to say.

Italo Calvino

When I get a little money, I buy books; and if there is any left I buy food and clothes.

Desiderius Erasmus

When you sell a man a book you don't sell him just twelve ounces of paper and ink and glue—you sell him a whole new life. Love and friendship and humor and ships at sea by night—there's all heaven and earth in a book, a real book I mean.

Christopher Morley

The mortality of inanimate things is terrible to me, but that of books most of all.

William Dean Howells

The man who does not read good books has no advantage over the man who can't read them.

Mark Twain

A truly great book should be read in youth, again in maturity, and once more in old age.

Robertson Davies

How many a man has dated a new era in his life from the reading of a book!

Henry David Thoreau

A book is like a garden carried in the pocket.

Chinese proverb

Books are the compass and telescopes and sextants and charts which other men have prepared to help us navigate the dangerous seas of human life.

Jesse Lee Bennett

Every book is, in an intimate sense, a circular letter to the friends of him who writes it.

Robert Louis Stevenson

Books may preach when the author cannot, when the author may not, when the author dares not, yea, and which is more, when the author is not.

Thomas Brooks

Books are bridges. The wisdom of bridges comes from the fact that they know both shores.

Mehmet Murat Ildan

One kind of good book should leave you asking: How did the author know that about me.

Alain De Botton

A good book is all-consuming: part of it becomes you, and part of you becomes it.

Wisława Szymborska

I suggest that the only books that influence us are those for which we are ready, and which have gone a little further down our particular path than we have yet gone ourselves.

E. M. Forster

If you only read the books that everyone else is reading, you can only think what everyone else is thinking.

Haruki Murakami

Books are keys to wisdom's treasure;
Books are paths that upward lead;
Books are gates to lands of pleasure
Books are friends,
Come, let us read.

An Unknown Book Lover

A good book makes you want to live inside
the story. A great book gives you no choice.

An Unknown Book Lover

A good book ... leaves you wanting to reread
the book. A great book compels you to reread
your own soul..

Richard Flanagan

All good books are alike in that they are truer
than if they had really happened.

Ernest Hemingway

The act of reading is a partnership. The
author builds a house, but the reader makes it
a home.

Jodi Picoult

Books are the carriers of civilization ... They
are companions, teachers, magicians, banks of

the treasures of the mind. Books are humanity
in print.

Barbara W. Tuchman

No two persons ever read the same book.

Edmund Wilson

Many a book is like a key to unknown
chambers within the castle of one's own self.

Franz Kafka

There is something wonderful about a book.
We can pick it up. We can heft it. We can read
it. We can set it down. We can think of what
we have read. It does something for us. We
can share minds, great actions and great
undertakings in the pages of a book.

Gordon B. Hinckley

Only in books has mankind known perfect
truth, love and beauty.

George Bernard Shaw

Reading a good book is like taking a journey.

Emma Gulliford

A good book is the precious lifeblood of a

master spirit, embalmed and treasured up on purpose to a life beyond life.

John Milton

Books are a uniquely portable magic.

Stephen King

There is no friend as loyal as a book.

Ernest Hemingway

A novel is like a bow, and the violin that produces the sound is the reader's soul.

Stendahl

A real book is not one that we read, but one that reads us.

Wystan Hugh Auden

I have lived a thousand lives and I've loved a thousand loves. I've walked on distant worlds and seen the end of time. Because I read.

George R. R. Martin

Books are many things: lullabies for the weary, ointment for the wounded, armor for the fearful, and nests for those in need of a home.

Glenda Millard

Books build a stairway to your imagination.

Stifyn Emrys

Books are, let's face it, better than everything else.

Nick Hornby

Books don't just go with you; they take you where you've never been.

An Unknown Book Lover

All good books are alike in that they are truer than if they had really happened and after you are finishing reading one you will feel that all that happened to you and afterwards it all belongs to you: the good and the bad, the ecstasy, the remorse and sorrow, the people and the places and how the weather was. If you can get so that you can give that to people, then you are a writer.

Ernest Hemingway

Books are no more threatened by Kindle than stairs by elevators.

Stephen Fry

A book you finish reading is not the same book it was before you read it.

David Mitchell

Handle a book the way a bee does a flower.
Extract its sweetness but do not damage it.

An Unknown Book Lover

Handle a book the way a bee does a flower.
Extract its sweetness but do not damage it.

An Unknown Book Lover

Thus I discovered what writers have always known (and have told us again and again): books always speak of other books, and every story tells a story that has already been told.

Umberto Eco

The reading of all good books is like a conversation with the finest minds of past centuries.

Rene Descartes

There are no faster or firmer friendships than those formed between people who love the same books.

Irving Stone

A book is a magic carpet that flies you off elsewhere. A book is a door. You open it You step through.

Jeanette Winterson

A book is a magical thing that lets you travel
to far-away places without ever leaving your
chair.

Katrina Mayer

What an astonishing thing a book is. It's a flat
object made from a tree with flexible parts on
which are imprinted lots of funny dark
squiggles. But one glance at it and you're
inside the mind of another person, maybe
somebody dead for thousands of years.
Across the millennia, an author is speaking
clearly and silently inside your head, directly to
you. Writing is perhaps the greatest of human
inventions, binding together people who
never knew each other, citizens of distant
epochs. Books break the shackles of time. A
book is proof that humans are capable of
working magic.

Carl Sagan

Great literature is simple language charged
with meaning to the utmost possible degree.

Ezra Pound

Books, I found, had the power to make time
stand still, retreat or fly into the future.

Jim Bishop

If you have a garden and a library you have
everything you need.

Cicero

Books are keys to wisdom's treasure
Books are gates to lands of pleasure
Books are paths that upward lead
Books are friends: come let us read.

Emilie Poulsson

The dearest ones of time, the strongest
friends of the soul—books.

Emily Dickinson

When reading, we don't fall in love with the
characters' appearance. We fall in love with
their words, their thoughts, and their hearts.
We fall in love with their souls.

An Unknown Book Lover

Books have a way of making you homesick
for a place you've never been to.

An Unknown Book Lover

If I died tonight, I can say that I have
travelled this whole world over and got lost in
many others. I have explored space, fought in
the Hunger Games with Katniss and defeated
Lord Voldemort with Harry. My life has been

full of magic and adventure because of one thing: books. They were the doors that took me anywhere and everywhere I wanted to go.

An Unknown Book Lover

Books may well be the only true magic.

Alice Hoffman

Books are the carriers of civilization. Without books, history is silent, literature dumb, science crippled, thought and speculation at a standstill.

Henry David Thoreau

A book is a dream that you hold in your hand.

Neil Gaiman

Books are the plane, and the train, and the road. They are the destination, and the journey. They are home.

Anna Quindlen

There is no friend as loyal as a book.

Ernest Hemingway

A book, too, can be a star, a living fire to lighten the darkness, leading out into the expanding universe.

Madeleine L'Engle

One must always be careful of books and what is inside them, for words have the power to change us.

Cassandra Clare

One kind of good book should leave you asking: how did the author know that about me?

Alain de Botton

Books are many things: lullabies for the weary, ointment for the wounded, armor for the fearful and nests for those in need of a home.

Glenda Millard

A classic is a book that has never finished what it has to say.

Italo Calvino

I believe that every book you read changes you; changes how you think, what you say, how you act, or how you look at the world. If a book doesn't change something about you then it has failed at being a book.

An Unknown Book Lover

My problem with reading books is that I get

distracted. By other books.

An Unknown Book Lover

The books we read answer questions we didn't even know existed.

Axel Marazzi

A book holds a house of gold.

Chinese proverb

A real book is not one that we read, but one that reads us.

Wystan Hugh Auden

That's the thing about books. They let you travel without moving your feet.

Jhumpa Lahiri

A well-composed book is a magic carpet on which we are wafted to a world that we cannot enter in any other way.

Caroline Gordon

A successful book is not made of what is in it, but what is left out of it.

Mark Twain

A book is like a garden carried in the pocket.

Chinese proverb

When you sell a man a book you don't sell him just twelve ounces of paper and ink and glue -- you sell him a whole new life. Love and friendship and humor and ships at sea by night—there's all heaven and earth in a book, a real book I mean.

Christopher Morley

My best friend is a person who will give me a book I have not read.

Abraham Lincoln

A well-composed book is a magic carpet on which we are wafted to a world that we cannot enter in any other way.

Caroline Gordon

Books are the compass and telescopes and sextants and charts which other men have prepared to help us navigate the dangerous seas of human life.

Jesse Lee Bennett

Of all the inanimate objects, of all men's creations, books are the nearest to us, for they contain our very thoughts, our ambitions, our indignations, our illusions, our fidelity to truth, and our persistent leaning toward error. But most of all they resemble us in the precarious hold on life.

Joseph Conrad

A book must be the axe for the frozen sea inside us.

Franz Kafka

Every book is, in an intimate sense, a circular letter to the friends of him who writes it.

Robert Louis Stevenson

Books have that strange quality, that being of the frailest and tenderest matter, they outlast brass, iron and marble.

William Drummond

All books are divisible into two classes, the books of the hour, and the books of all time.

John Ruskin

In the best books great men talk to us, give us their most precious thoughts, and pour their souls into ours.

William Ellery Channing

A book is like a vacation for the brain.

Rachel Adams

A book, too, can be a star, explosive material, capable of stirring up fresh life endlessly, a living fire to lighten the darkness, leading out into the expanding universe.

Madeleine L'Engle

Books are many things: lullabies for the weary, ointment for the wounded, armor for the fearful and nests for those in need of a home.

Glenda Millard

Many a book is like a key to unknown chambers within the castle of one's own self.

Franz Kafka

There is something wonderful about a book. We can pick it up. We can heft it. We can read it. We can set it down. We can think of what we have read. It does something for us. We can share minds, great actions and great undertakings in the pages of a book.

Gordon B. Hinckley

Who said time machines haven't been built yet? They already exist. They're called books.

Robert Benchley

On rare occasions there comes along a profound original, an odd little book that appears out of nowhere, from the pen of some obscure storyteller, and once you have read it, you will never go completely back to where you were before. The kind of book you might hesitate to lend for fear you might miss its company. The kind of book that echoes from the heart of some ancient knowing, and whispers from time's forgotten cave that life may be more than it seems, and less.

Edmund J. Banfield

A good book makes you want to live inside the story. A great book gives you no choice.

An Unknown Book Lover

"OK, just one more chapter ..."

Book lovers everywhere

Other Books by Rocky Henriques

Be sure to pick up the companion volume to *The Book Lover's Book of Quotes*, which is entitled *The Writer's Book of Quotes*.

Please visit
http://amzn.to/2hlGsoZ

for a complete listing
of all available books

About The Author

Rocky Henriques has pastored churches in Mississippi since 1979. He earned a Master of Divinity degree and a Doctor of Ministry degree from New Orleans Baptist Theological Seminary. Rocky has two adult children, Jennifer and Jonathan, and two grandchildren, Emma Claire and Joshua. He lives in Mississippi with his beautiful wife Sharon, a rowdy parrot named Kermit, and two spoiled dogs, Emmy and Gabi.